THE FIRING
ON
FORT SUMTER
A Splintered Nation Goes to War

THE FIRING
ON
FORT SUMTER
A Splintered Nation Goes to War

Nancy A. Colbert

MORGAN
REYNOLDS
Incorporated

Greensboro

THE FIRING ON FORT SUMTER
A SPLINTERED NATION GOES TO WAR

Copyright © 2001 by Nancy A. Colbert

Picture credits: Courtesy of the Library of Congress

Library of Congress Cataloging-in-Publication Data

Colbert, Nancy A.
   The firing on Fort Sumter: a splintered nation goes to war / Nancy A. Colbert.
      p. cm.
   Includes bibliographical references (p.) and index.
   ISBN 1-883846-51-X (lib. bdg.)
      1. Fort Sumter (Charleston, S.C.)--Seige, 1861--Juvenile literature. 2. Charleston
   (S.C.)--History--Civil War, 1861-1865--Juvenile literature. 3. United
   States--History--Civil War, 1861-1865--Juvenle literature. [1. Fort Sumter (Charleston,
   S.C.)--Seige, 1861. 2. Charleston (S.C.)--History--Civil War, 1861-1865. 3. United
   States--History--Civil War, 1861-1865--Campaigns.] I. Title. II. Series.

   E471.1 .C65 2000
   973.7'31--dc21
                                                                            00-041874

Printed in the United States of America
First Edition

To my husband, Jim,
and to all of our family;

with special thanks
to my editor at Morgan Reynolds, John Riley,

and to Karen Colbert, Barbara Kramer, Linda Skeers
my readers and encouragers.

Contents

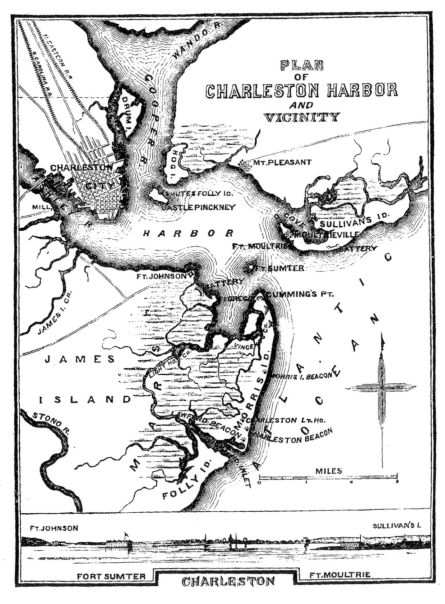

Charleston Harbor

Chapter One

If We Neglect
to Strengthen Ourselves

In December 1860, U.S. Army Major Robert Anderson had to make a decision. His small garrison was stationed in old Fort Moultrie, located on the northeast shore of the harbor of Charleston, South Carolina.

Perched on the sea front of Sullivan's Island, just off the mainland, the fort had been built to defend the citizens of Charleston during the War of 1812. Over the years, wind and waves had gradually built a ramp of sand to the top of the sixteen-foot brick walls, and now the fort sat down in the sand dunes. A child could climb up the backside of the dunes and walk right into the fort. Occasionally, a cow grazing on the scrubby growth dropped in for an unexpected visit. Over the years, visitors from the summer cottages along the beach had developed the habit of strolling in and out of the fort at will.

For decades this easy access had not been a concern. The fort had been built to defend the people who summered in the fine cottages from sea front attack. The civilians and soldiers had entertained one another at dances and parties. In contrast to being assigned to some dusty, lonely, and dangerous station in Indian country, troops and officers had considered service at Fort Moultrie an easy assignment.

Now all had changed. The citizens of Charleston called the U. S. soldiers "the enemy." Years of controversy and fighting over extending slavery into the new territories had driven the United States to the brink of an explosion. The epicenter of the coming conflict was Charleston, where those who were most fiercely dedicated to the cause of splintering the United States were called "Fire-Eaters." These same people were so hostile toward the federal troops that Major Anderson had ordered the gates of the fort closed. Anderson felt that his position was like "a sheep tied watching the butcher sharpen a knife to cut his throat."

Infuriated by the election of Abraham Lincoln of Illinois to be the sixteenth president, South Carolina had seceded from the United States on December 20, 1860. The political leaders of the state, such as Governor Francis Pickens and Charleston newspaper editor Robert Rhett, had insisted that the election of the "Black Republicans" to power had severed the national bonds formed almost eighty years before. The vote to leave the union, taken in the state capital of Columbia, had been unanimous. As soon as the vote for secession had been cast, Charlestonians began demanding that all of the U.S.

Army Major Robert Anderson faced the dilemma to either stay put in an indefensible fort or move his men and their families to safety at Fort Sumter and risk civil war.

military installations located in and around the harbor be turned over to state authorities. They insisted that the three forts rightfully belonged to South Carolina and requested that the "foreign" soldiers now manning them leave.

The commander of the forts, Major Anderson, was a lean man with graying hair. An artillery expert and graduate of West Point Military Academy, he was a reasonable, religious man of Virginian ancestry who was born in Kentucky. His wife was from Georgia. He had owned a few slaves himself. President Buchanan had appointed Anderson to his command because he knew that Anderson would be cautious.

Although he was of southern heritage, Anderson had taken an oath to serve his country. He did not think South Carolina, or any state, had the right to break away from the Union. His loyalty to his country never faltered. A kinsman of his said, "The Ten Commandments, the Constitution of the United States, and the Army Regulations were his guides in life."

Anderson and his men inhabited Fort Moultrie, which had fifty-five guns. Tiny Castle Pinckney, located nearest to the city's battery on a tiny spit of land, had eighteen guns and four howitzers. The largest fort was unfinished Sumter, situated at the mouth of the harbor. Sumter had seventy-eight guns, although almost all of them were yet unmounted.

After taking command on November 15, 1860, Major

Anderson had inspected each of the forts. At Fort Moultrie, he discovered that some guns had been dismounted to make way for repairs, leaving gaps in the walls. The wooden structures inside, including quarters, hospital, and storehouses, would burn easily. Construction planking on the outside of the fort could provide handy ladders for invaders.

Anderson had to decide whether to stay in Moultrie and face almost certain violent eviction by the South Carolinians or to relocate his small garrison to Sumter, the most defensible position.

Major Anderson's decision was made more difficult by the orders he had received when he took over the command. He was to defend the forts but avoid a collision with the people of South Carolina. The orders also said he was "authorized to take steps whenever you have tangible evidence . . . of a hostile act." Anderson thought his orders vague. What actions could he possibly take, short of surrender, that would not create a conflict with the Charlestonians? They would certainly view a relocation to Sumter as a hostile act. On the other hand, was he free to determine that the almost daily speeches and editorials that advocated the citizens take the forts by force were hostile acts that justified him moving his troops to the safer fort?

Anderson soon realized that he could not hope for much guidance from his superiors in Washington. The current president, James Buchanan, would remain in power until Lincoln was inaugurated on March 4, 1861. It became clear to Anderson that his superiors in Washington were as confused as to what was the proper course of action as he was.

On November 24, 1860, Anderson asked Secretary of War Floyd for reinforcements. "If we neglect to strengthen ourselves, South Carolina will most assuredly attack us," he wrote. But Floyd, a citizen of Virginia, said if he reinforced the Charleston forts, South Carolina might think they were preparing for war. He refused the request.

Convinced that Floyd simply did not understand the danger of his situation, Anderson repeated his request for reinforcements on November 28 and again on December 1. He asked for at least two companies for Sumter and Pinckney, and reinforcements for Fort Moultrie and additional ordnance stores (military weapons). He believed that, with this amount of strength, South Carolina would not attempt to take the forts.

Finally, Secretary of War Floyd sent him reinforcement: one man, Lieutenant R. K. Meade, a Virginian. This tepid response helped Major Anderson make his decision. He now knew that he could not stay in Fort Moultrie. It was indefensible to even the slightest attack. Even a single sharpshooter could kill or wound his men from atop one of the high dunes or from the upper windows of the summer cottages. His first duty was to protect the soldiers who served under him. Anderson determined to move his troops. He would do it quietly and on his own. Then he would inform his superiors in Washington.

Major Anderson's senior officers at Fort Sumter included his second in command, Captain Abner Doubleday. Years earlier, after watching kids playing aimlessly with bats and balls, Doubleday had devised a scoring system that eventually led to the game of baseball. Captain John Foster was an engineer who answered to engineering headquarters in Washington rather than to Anderson. The major also commanded Captain Truman Seymour and Surgeon Captain Samuel Crawford. The four junior officers were First Lieutenant Theodore Talbot of Company II, a Kentuckian; First Lieutenant Jefferson C. Davis, an Indianian who had come up through the ranks; First Lieutenant George Snyder, Corps of Engineers, a New York Stater who had won top honors at West Point; and Second Lieutenant Norman Hall, a young man from Michigan, who served as quartermaster and adjutant.

Major Anderson chose Christmas Day for the move. The people of Charleston would be celebrating not only the Christian holidays but also the first Christmas of their new republic. He kept his plans secret, though, because many of his soldiers lived in quarters in the nearby town of Moultrieville. He did want to risk his plans being leaked.

He ordered his quartermaster, Second Lieutenant Hall, to secure two large barges, called *lighters*. Normally, these boats hauled workmen and building supplies to Fort

Sumter and Castle Pinckney. Lieutenant Hall, who was a recent graduate of West Point, was the "kid" of the outfit.

Major Anderson told Hall that the reason he needed the lighters was because he wanted the wives and children of the soldiers taken to the safety of old abandoned Fort Johnson on James Island across the harbor. He said that if Fort Moultrie were attacked, they would be safe there.

On Christmas Day, the boats were secured at a sea wall near Fort Moultrie. Then a cold winter rain moved in, blowing across the harbor. Major Anderson could not carry out his plans that day. It would have been too miserable out in the harbor in open boats.

The day after Christmas dawned clear. Lieutenant Hall had the lighters ready to, as he thought, move the forty-five wives and children to Fort Johnson.

Then Major Anderson told Hall the true plan. Hall was to pretend he was taking them to Fort Johnson but not to land. When he heard a two-gun signal, he was to run the boats for Fort Sumter.

In addition to the wives and children, four months' provisions for everyone and personal belongings were added to the boats before they were shoved off into the harbor.

The other officers had not yet been told of the plans. Anderson had some doubts about a few of his men. The officer he had the most doubts about was Lieutenant Meade, who worked with Lieutenant George Snyder on the ongoing construction project at Fort Sumter. When the two officers asked Anderson how they were to haul their workmen and building supplies when Hall was using the lighters to ferry the women and children, Major Anderson told them the real plan. Meade, from Virginia, was angry. He had a Southerner's sympathy for South Carolina and thought the plan was an affront to the state, but he obeyed the major's orders.

The day passed and Anderson continued to deal with everyone on a "need to know" basis until, at the early winter dusk, Captain Doubleday came to invite Major Anderson to tea. Major Anderson shocked him with his reply: "Captain, in twenty minutes you will leave with your company for Fort Sumter."

At 5:00 P.M. Major Anderson rolled the garrison's flag and put it under his arm. Then he led his assembled men silently out of Fort Moultrie. Captain Foster and Surgeon Samuel Crawford, along with seven enlisted men and four non-commissioned officers, were left behind in the fort as a rear guard.

In the gathering dusk, Major Anderson's small garrison quietly walked pass Moultrieville, where South Carolina militiamen were having supper. They marched down to a small cove where three, six-oared barges waited and quickly climbed into the boats.

Anderson was in charge of the first boatload, Meade the second, and Doubleday the last. They shoved off. They had to hurry because the South Carolina guard boats that had begun to patrol the harbor waters would soon begin their nightly runs. A full moon rose as they rowed toward the distant edge of the harbor. Unfinished Fort Sumter grew larger as they neared the tiny island of sea shells and scrap granite that had been built on top of a sandbar decades before, when the new nation was united together to protect its shores from foreign attack. To keep the people of Charleston from suspecting his move, Major Anderson had ordered Captain Foster not to mount Sumter's cannon.

Back at Fort Moultrie, the scholarly Surgeon Captain Crawford and the engineer Captain Foster trained two of the fort's biggest guns, the Columbiads, on the channel. Through a telescope they watched the tiny boats inching across the harbor. Their orders were to fire on the South Carolina guard boats if they attempted to interfere with the garrison's crossing.

Near the halfway mark, the troops in the boats spotted a guard boat chugging out from Charleston. Anderson and Meade circled their boats away from the guard boat. But Doubleday decided to make a run for Fort Sumter. He ordered his men to take off their army greatcoats with their shiny brass buttons and to cover their guns so the bright moon would not glint off them. He took off his large black hat decorated with a plume.

A hundred yards away, the guard boat slowed then drifted to a stop, idle paddle wheels dripping. Back at Fort Moultrie, Foster and Crawford got the guard boat in the

Federal troops and their families rowed to Fort Sumter under the cloak of night.

sights of the two Columbiads. They prepared to fire. Then the guard boat's paddle wheels began to turn again and the steamer chugged away.

Doubleday raced for Fort Sumter, the men rowing as fast as they could. Anderson and Meade turned and followed Doubleday. When the three boats landed on the esplanade, the flat open stretch along the shore in front of Fort Sumter, the troops climbed out and formed rank.

As they marched into the fort, the civilian workers who camped there were surprised and frightened to see soldiers march in out of the night. A few Unionists among the workmen cheered, but most of the men, natives of Charleston, sided with the secessionists. They muttered angrily at the Union soldiers.

A pre-arranged, two gun signal was fired. Out in the harbor, Hall, who had held back with the women and children to avoid any conflict, heard the long-awaited signal with joy. He headed his boats toward Fort Sumter, where the soldiers met their tired but happy families at the water's edge.

Meanwhile at Fort Moultrie, the soldiers under Captain Foster's direction spiked the cannons left behind by driving long, thick pieces of wood into the guns' vents. This rendered them temporarily useless. He burned the gun carriages so the secessionists could not use them. Captain Foster also destroyed all of the ammunition he could not bring with him. Their last task was to cut the flagstaff down, to avoid the secessionists from hoisting the South Carolina state flag over the fort. As they worked, they remained vigilant, watching for attack.

In the early morning of December 27, the boats left Sumter and went back to Fort Moultrie for the remaining Union soldiers. Surgeon Captain Crawford loaded all the medical equipment and supplies he could into the boats. Then the last of the Union army evacuated Fort Moultrie and headed for Fort Sumter.

The garrison now held a fort surrounded by water, one they could defend. Major Anderson believed that both the North and the South would be thankful he had made his move. He reported to the Secretary of War's adjutant general, Colonel Cooper:

Colonel:

I have the honor to report that I have just completed, by the blessing of God, the removal to this fort [Fort Sumter] all of my garrison . . . We have one year's supply of hospital stores and about four months' supply of provisions for my command . . . The step which I have taken was, in my opinion, necessary to prevent the effusion of blood.

But Anderson's move, which was meant to protect the peace, served as a rallying cry for war in the North. In the South the move was called even worse. The *Charleston Courier* shouted: "Maj. Robert Anderson, U.S.A., has achieved the unenviable distinction of opening civil war."

Chapter Two

O. P. F.

In Washington on December 27, President Buchanan received the news from an old friend that Major Anderson had moved to Fort Sumter. Senator Jefferson Davis of Mississippi hurried into the president's office. The future president of the Confederacy asked Buchanan if he had received any messages from Charleston in the last three hours. "None," Buchanan replied.

"Then I have a great calamity to announce to you," Davis said. He told the president of Anderson's move and concluded by saying, "You are surrounded with blood and dishonor on all sides."

Davis demanded that Buchanan order Anderson to return to Fort Moultrie. He called the move a "reinforcement" of Sumter and an act of aggression. Buchanan responded politely to Davis's comments and refused to commit himself to any action. He said that he wanted to wait for more information.

This was how the president responded to most requests. He preferred delaying decisions as long as possible. President James Buchanan of Pennsylvania was known by both his supporters and his detractors as "O. P. F." His friends meant the letters to stand for "Old Public Functionary." His enemies said that it was an abbreviation for "Old Pennsylvania Fogy."

On November 9, three days after Lincoln's election, President Buchanan had called a meeting of his cabinet. He emphasized that the country faced a momentous problem. It seemed as though the United States was coming apart. It grieved him that this was happening while he was president. He proposed a convention of all the states in the hopes of working out a compromise that would hold the nation together. Then he added that he also planned to say in his annual message to Congress that the federal government had the legal power to maintain the Union by force if necessary.

The cabinet erupted into an argument. Stout, shaggy, and rumpled, Secretary of the Treasury Howell Cobb of Georgia protested passionately that the states had the right to secede. Secretary of the Interior Jacob Thompson from Mississippi denounced the plan, too. Secretly, he was anxious for his state to secede. He was already sending confidential information to his secessionist friends and planned to have an active role in the new southern republic.

John Floyd, Secretary of War, also had strong secessionist leanings. At the time of the meeting, he was negotiating the sale of 10,000 muskets to South Carolina.

Although South Carolina was still a state at that time and legally could buy the guns, Floyd was well aware that the weapons could end up in the hands of soldiers fighting the United States. He was also working to ship a load of cannon to Mississippi.

On the other side of the issue, Secretary of State Lewis Cass of Michigan, said the secession doctrine was illegal and supported Buchanan's decision to say so publicly. Attorney General Jeremiah Black wanted to send a strong force to the Charleston forts right away to protect them from the South Carolina "Fire-Eaters." Cass and Black, firm believers in Union principles, also supported Buchanan's call for a unifying convention.

Isaac Toucey, the Secretary of the Navy, was a weak-willed man who seconded whatever Buchanan suggested. Postmaster General Joseph Holt backed Buchanan's ideas but did not want a convention because he was afraid it would fail and only encourage the secessionists.

Because the cabinet was divided into secessionist and anti-secessionist groups, and the president resisted making a decision without the political support of the cabinet, Buchanan did little in the weeks immediately after Lincoln's election.

President Buchanan, sixty-nine years old, tired, and infirm, had become known as a "Doughface": a slang expression for a northerner with southern sympathies. He remained loyal to the Union, however, he thought the slave states had been pushed to the brink of war by radical abolitionists who demanded an end to slavery. He was

President Buchanan wished to avoid any skirmishes until the end of his term.

also a Democrat, and the incoming president was the first elected from the new Republican Party.

Buchanan had run for the presidency in 1856 on a platform that supported slavery in the states where it then existed. He also thought that slavery should be allowed to expand into the territories. He had won the office with strong southern support and had rewarded the South by placing many prominent leaders from slave states in his cabinet.

After his election, Buchanan, who had served in several high-level positions including Secretary of State and Ambassador to Great Britian, was swept away by the rush of events. Kansas had erupted into violence as anti-slavery and pro-slavery settlers burned and murdered in a struggle to win the territory to their side. Many, on both sides of the issue, saw the fighting in Kansas as a prelude to the coming war.

In 1857, the Supreme Court had ruled in *Dred Scott v. Sandford* that slaves had no rights of citizenship. It also stated that because slaves were "property," it was unconstitutional for Congress to deny slave owners from taking slaves into the territories. To do so would infringe on property rights protected in the Fifth Amendment. This decision, which attempted to deny the federal government any control over the expansion of slavery, dismayed and infuriated many in the North.

Tensions continued to build during Buchanan's term. There was a financial panic in 1857, setting off a string of bankruptcies and creating a climate of fear and economic uncertainity. Riots erupted when northern states refused to return runaway slaves to their southern masters, and abolitionists were jailed for inciting slave protesters to attack federal marshalls attempting to arrest runaways.

The climatic event that pushed the debate to the point of no return was John Brown's raid on the federal arsenal in Harpers Ferry, Virginia. Brown, a fierce, Bible-quoting abolitionist who had murdered pro-slavery settlers in Kansas, planned to seize the weapons stored at the arsenal and disperse them to slaves. He hoped these slaves would escape and form a guerilla army under his command in the Virginia hills. Brown and his group were captured by troops led by Colonel Robert E. Lee. They were tried and executed. Brown provided secessionist southerners with an example of northern treachery, and for the abolitionists, he became a martyr.

It was clear by early 1860 that the upcoming election was crucial. If the Republicans elected the next president, regardless of who he was, several southern states would leave the Union. When the Democratic Party fell apart because of sectional tensions within its ranks and nominated both a southern and a northern candidate for president at two separate conventions (one of which was held in Charleston), it assured Republican candidate Abraham Lincoln's election on November 6, 1860. Within days after the election, South Carolina voted to hold a state convention to debate secession. No one doubted that the convention would vote to leave the Union.

After the election, President Buchanan had four more months in office, and more than anything else, he wanted to avoid war. The rush of events in the last four years had left him exhausted. When, in October, old Winfield Scott, the commanding general of the Army of the United States and hero of the War of 1812, had warned him that the southern states were going to seize all of the federal forts, Buchanan was filled with despair. Scott said that all of the forts should be reinforced, but the tiny U. S. Army had only 16,000 regular troops, and they were busy in the western Indian country. It would be impossible to adequately garrison the southern forts, even if Buchanan had the heart to do so.

Scott suggested taking measures to enlarge the army, but Buchanan was afraid to do anything that might be interpreted as threatening to the South. Buchanan was convinced that many southerners were still strong Union supporters, and he did not want to push them over to the secessionist side by any aggressive actions. This tension between trying to defend the forts and working to minimize the number of states that left the Union was a factor in every decision Buchanan—and Lincoln—would make in the next five months.

The Charleston forts were only three of the nine federal coastal forts in the South. From the beginning, however, they were in the eye of the political storm—especially

Sumter, which was situated in a strategic harbor location and four times larger than Fort Moultrie. The United States government had spent thirty years and a million dollars building the pentagonal fort. It was designed for a garrison of 650 men and 146 guns and would be a stronghold if it were ever finished. Incomplete walls left openings at ground level that provided easy entrance. Sixty-six guns, 5,600 shot and shell, piles of sand, masonry, and equipment littered the parade ground. Building materials were stacked everywhere inside the fort, along the wharf, and the shore.

The fort was designed for three tiers with 146 guns, but as of yet, only three guns were mounted on the upper tier, one gun on the second, and eleven on the lower. One advantage for Anderson and his men was that few South Carolinians knew how unfinished the fort was.

Over the next weeks, Buchanan's government began to fall apart. On December 13, Secretary of State Cass, again, strongly urged him to reinforce the Charleston forts, but Buchanan refused. Cass did not know that the president had made an unofficial bargain with the governor of South Carolina not to send reinforcements if the South Carolinians promised not to seize federal property. When Cass learned of this agreement, he resigned in anger. Attorney General Jeremiah Black was then appointed Secretary of State.

From the Union perspective, the humiliations continued. On December 17, Captain Foster of Fort Moultrie needed some muskets. He was entitled to forty under an unfilled ordnance order, so he and a detachment of U.S. soldiers obtained the guns and ammunition from the federal arsenal located in the city of Charleston.

South Carolinians erupted in anger. They said that Foster's act violated the president's promise not to reinforce the Charleston forts. Angry messages went to Washington, D.C., and Secretary Floyd telegraphed Captain Foster and told him to return the guns to the arsenal. Union supporters felt this was another humiliation.

In the meantime, Charlestonians worked throughout December installing guns around the harbor. Men, supplies, and ammunition churned past Fort Moultrie. The *Charleston Mercury* insisted in editorials that South Carolina should take Fort Sumter immediately. The South Carolina legislature supported taking possession of all the harbor forts.

Charleston was teeming with supporters of secession, most of whom had no official capacity. They were simply drawn to what had become the heart of the secessionists movement. The most flamboyant supporter was sixty-year-old Edmund Ruffin, an eccentric Virginian who had made a fortune developing a manure-based fertilizer. He had waged a one-man campaign to restore the soil of his beloved region, teaching his fellow planters how to keep their land from wearing out. Fanatically pro-slavery, he was much more interested in secession than fertilizer and had long predicted war between the North and the South.

Captain Abner Doubleday was second in command at Fort Sumter.

In South Carolina, Ruffin found the militia marching and bands playing. The people of South Carolina were "statriots" (those who put their own state before the United States) not patriots, he said. Ruffin's eyes blazed. His long white hair whipped about his shoulders. In one speech he even took credit for secession. "This [secession] has been the one great idea of my life," he said soon after his arrival.

The day after the state convention voted to secede was declared a holiday in Charleston. The Stars and Stripes came down and the state palmetto flag was hoisted over the city. The *Mercury* shouted: "The tea had been thrown overboard, the revolution of 1860 has been initiated." This reminded the people of the Boston Tea Party that helped start the American Revolution. The South Carolina legislature authorized the governor to spend $100,000 for arms. The U.S. senators from South Carolina resigned their seats.

In Charleston, the judge of the United States District Court in Charleston stood up, tossed off his judicial gown, and said, "So far as I am concerned, the Temple of Justice, raised under the Constitution of the United States, is now closed."

Emotions ran strong outside of the South as well. In Washington, Lewis Cass, former Secretary of State, said that the secession of South Carolina was monstrous. "The people of the South are mad; the people in the North are asleep; the President is pale with fear . . . God only knows what is to be the fate of my country."

It was only a matter of time before the other states of the Deep South followed South Carolina. The only question was what would the states of the upper south, such as Virginia and North Carolina, and the border states of Maryland, Kentucky and Missouri would do. Many of the leaders of these states warned the federal government not to use arms against South Carolina. This seemed to immobilize the federal government, and some secessionist leaders became convinced that war could be avoided. Ex-Senator Chesnut of South Carolina said that he thought the southern states would be able to leave peacefully. "I will drink all the blood shed in the war," he said.

President Buchanan hoped that Chestnut was right. But he had little faith that extremists on both sides would not find a way to bring on the war they had long advocated. He just hoped that it would not happen before Lincoln was inaugurated on March 4, 1860.

Then news came of Major Anderson's unexpected move to Fort Sumter, and the newspapers and halls of government were filled with suggestions on what the president should do next. Various northern leaders advised the president to reinforce Anderson, move him back to Fort Moultrie, remove him from Charleston, hand over the forts, or send war vessels. Buchanan, a life-long bachelor, walked the lonely halls of the White House muttering, "The forts, the forts, what must I do about the forts?"

Chapter Three

He Still Commands the Harbor

The outrage President Buchanan faced in Washington on December 27 was more than equaled by the riot of emotions that swept over Charleston and Fort Sumter on that chilly morning. After a busy night of moving, the federal soldiers lined the fort's ramparts and cheered as a South Carolina steamer passed by. The southern militiamen on the steamer gasped at the sight of the Yankees in the disputed fort.

Afterward, Anderson's garrison gathered on the parade ground that was littered with construction materials, unmounted guns, and supplies. The major marched out with the U.S. flag he had carried over from Fort Moultrie. Then the chaplin, Reverend Mattias Harris, offered a prayer that this flag would soon fly over a united country. Anderson knelt with a bowed head.

The soldiers raised the flag. The Stars and Stripes flew over Fort Sumter. The band played "Hail Columbia" as the flag snapped in the breeze. The men cheered again and again. They now had a fort they could defend.

Almost simultaneously, the South Carolina guard ship's sirens wailed and burned blue lights to alert the people of Charleston that the Yankees they thought safely sealed in old Fort Moultrie had sneaked out in the dead of night and "seized" Fort Sumter. Surely this was an act of war! The South Carolinians shot rockets into the sky from lookout stations.

Governor Pickens sent two men to Fort Sumter. They rowed out and presented their calling card. Major Anderson received them hospitably. The visitors informed Anderson that he had violated an understanding between President Buchanan and Governor Pickens not to reinforce Fort Sumter and said that he should return to Fort Moultrie.

Anderson said he was not aware of any understanding, and that he had not reinforced Fort Sumter, only moved there. He did not intend to return to Fort Moultrie.

Angry, Governor Pickens sent three South Carolina companies to take over Castle Pinckney. Ordnance Sergeant Skillen, the sole guard, closed the gates, but the angry militiamen climbed over the walls on scaling ladders and poured into the fort. The dark blue Palmetto flag of South Carolina, with its white crescent and palm tree, was then raised over the tiny fort. Two hundred men also landed on Sullivan's Island and took over empty Fort Moultrie.

The installations were federal property, and technically, these actions were acts of war. Major Anderson and his officers watched with growing indignation from the parapet of Fort Sumter. Then Anderson sent Lieutenant Hall to Moultrie to ask the men who had given them authority to occupy the forts. Colonel Wilmot DeSaussure said that his orders came from the governor of the sovereign state of South Carolina. The Palmetto troops also occupied dilapidated Fort Johnson on James Island.

Captain F. C. Humphreys, Military Storekeeper of Ordnance, was in charge of the federal arsenal in Charleston when the South Carolina militiamen came on December 30. The inexperienced militiamen aimed loaded guns at Humphreys and his men. Behind them was an arsenal full of ammunition. Before the angry militiamen could accidentally detonate the powder, Captain Humphreys surrendered. The South Carolinians seized 22,000 muskets, cannons, and large quantities of ammunition.

The South Carolina militia also seized Captain Foster's engineering office in Charleston. There they found all of the maps and diagrams of the forts in the Charleston harbor. By January 1, 1861, Fort Sumter was the only Charleston fort left in federal control.

While the citizens of South Carolina were taking events into their own hands, the political leaders in Washington continued to have meetings and to argue. The same day that Anderson moved to Fort Sumter, three South Carolina commissioners came to Washington. They wanted the Charleston forts turned over to South

South Carolina Governor Pickens ordered the seizure of the remaining forts in Charleston Harbor after Major Anderson moved his garrison to Fort Sumter.

Carolina and all Union forces out of the harbor. The president refused to meet with them on an official basis. He did not want to give the appearance of recognizing South Carolina as being an independent republic with official ambassadors. Buchanan decided to call another cabinet meeting.

During the meeting, Secretary of War Floyd became furious. He said that Anderson had disobeyed orders and made war inevitable by moving to Sumter. He insisted that President Buchanan order Anderson back to Fort Moultrie. Secretary of State Black, a former judge who was a strong man but always appeared untidy with his crooked wig and too-small clothes, said that Anderson had not disobeyed orders. His orders had authorized him to take the necessary steps to protect his garrison. Black believed the forts should be reinforced. Edwin Stanton, the new attorney general, backed Black. "A President of the United States who would make such an order (to remove Major Anderson's garrison back to Fort Moultrie) would be guilty of treason," Stanton snapped.

Floyd continued to insist President Buchanan had given a pledge to South Carolina not to reinforce Sumter. The quarrel grew violent and hot words flew. After midnight, the cabinet voted four to three against ordering Anderson back to Fort Moultrie. Buchanan still delayed his decision. He said he wanted to wait for official word from Anderson informing the president of the move to Sumter before he told the major that he could stay.

The next cabinet meeting uncovered a conspiracy that undercut the supporters of secession. As a weary Floyd lay on a sofa of the cabinet room, he heard Stanton charge that a million dollars worth of bonds had been stolen from the Treasury. Floyd knew that the dark story of his shady dealings was coming out.

Floyd, a careless and disorganized man, was responsible for thousands of dollars of government funds. He kept many of his records on scraps of paper, which he sometimes lost. In addition, he had given away Indian Trust Fund bonds worth $870,000 to a company that delivered supplies to frontier army posts. He had done it to cover the losses of the company, which was owned by a friend.

Now that these underhanded dealings were revealed, Floyd had to be dismissed from the cabinet. Buchanan, who hated confrontations, told the vice-president to fire him. But Floyd refused to resign. Secretaries Black and Stanton were outraged that he refused to leave.

Finally, on Dec. 29, Floyd resigned. In his resignation letter he said that he was acting to protest the president's breaking of his pledge to South Carolina not to reinforce Fort Sumter. Floyd then returned to Virginia, where he was honored at banquets and made pro-secession speeches.

Joseph Holt, a strong Unionist, replaced Floyd. One of Holt's first commands was to reverse an order of his predecessor that would have sent 124 cannon to Mississippi.

Senator Louis T. Wigfall of Texas, a former South Carolinian, telegraphed the general of the South Carolina military. "Holt succeeds Floyd. It means war. Cut off supplies from Anderson and take Sumter soon as possible."

Former Assistant Secretary of State, William Trescot, who was now serving as South Carolina's agent in Washington, met with the commissioners from South Carolina. When Trescot, who had been born in Charleston, was Assistant Secretary of State, he had kept South Carolina informed of all the activities of the cabinet. Trescot also sent a warning to South Carolina Governor Pickens about Holt replacing Floyd.

In the meantime, Colonel Sam Colt, a firearms manufacturer, busily shipped boatloads of guns to South Carolina. He defended himself by reminding people that the president had said that South Carolina remained a part of the Union. Why couldn't he sell them guns? Another Connecticut munitions manufacturer felt the same way. He sold 300,000 pounds of powder to South Carolina.

In Washington, the line between friends and enemies was blurred. Cabinet members and elected members of Congress could be—and were—working against the government they were elected to serve. The senators from Alabama, Georgia, Florida, Louisiana, Texas, and Mississippi met and agreed to keep their United States Senate seats as long as possible to "keep President Buchanan's hands tied."

Secretary of War John Floyd resigned after it was discovered he had embezzled government funds.

The commissioners from South Carolina continued to ask for the Charleston forts. Attorney General Stanton raged at the president, telling him he could not deal with these men. They were traitors, not ambassadors, he insisted. Any president that dealt with them was a president who could be impeached.

Secretary of State Black wrote a letter for the president to give the commissioners:

"The forts in the harbor of Charleston belong to this Government, are its own, and cannot be given up . . . He [Major Anderson] has saved the country, I solemnly believe. He has done everything that mortal man could do to repair the fatal error which the administration committed in not sending enough troops to hold *all* the forts. He has kept the strongest one. He still commands the harbor."

Frustrated, Howell Cobb of Georgia resigned from the cabinet and returned home. Floyd was gone. Thompson of Mississippi was helpless. Buchanan's was at last a united Union cabinet. Strengthened, the president made his decision. He sent the firm reply to the South Carolina commissioners. They could not have the forts. Major Anderson would stay at Fort Sumter.

The commissioners accused the president of breaking his pledge and of choosing war over peace. They left for South Carolina. Senator Jefferson Davis and several others attacked the president in the newspapers. President Buchanan, finally growing stubborn in the face of the

Attorney General Edwin Stanton fiercely defended the Union against secessionists.

insults, said: "It is all now over and reinforcements must be sent."

Trescot scurried to report to his South Carolina contacts. He had heard that the *Harriet Lane*, a revenue cutter (a lightly armed boat used to collect revenue), was being sent to Sumter with reinforcements. Senator Hunter of Virginia told Trescot: "Telegraph at once to your people to sink vessels in the channel of the harbor." The plan was to seal the harbor with the hulls of sunken ships.

At Sumter, Anderson felt he was merely an army major who had tried to put his men in a secure position so the South Carolinians would not walk in and seize control. But when newspapers and mail began arriving, the major and his men discovered they had made headlines in northern newspapers. They were heroes. Anderson was shocked by stories calling him a military genius.

The soldiers knew they represented the United States government in a hostile harbor. With the aid of the few construction workers who chose to stay, the soldiers went to work. They plugged the holes in the walls, mounted guns, and hoisted the heavy cannon into place with makeshift pulleys and levers. They even managed to raise a 15,400-pound cannon to a platform high above the ground. Then the soldiers carried the cannon balls, which weighed 128 pounds each, up the steps one-by-one and piled them by the big cannon. They worked harder than they had ever planned to do, but the soldiers were happy they had made the move to Fort Sumter and had a good fort to defend.

The four months' food supplies the garrison had hauled from Fort Moultrie did not include any fresh meat and vegetables, so Major Anderson sent Lieutenant Snyder and some men to Charleston for fresh provisions. The men rowed over to the city.

When they arrived, their boat was seized. The South Carolinians would not allow them to buy any fresh provisions. Later, the men were let go and allowed to return to Fort Sumter empty handed. The salted and dried provisions would have to do.

While the United States soldiers worked to prepare Fort Sumter, South Carolina defense preparations at former Fort Moultrie sped up. The militia built new gun carriages to replace the ones Captain Foster and his men had burned. The spiked guns were repaired.

On Morris Island, directly across the harbor from Fort Sumter to the south, South Carolina men began to erect a battery of heavy artillery. With Morris Island fortified, the South Carolinians could fire on any large vessel that might try to come to assist or to supply Fort Sumter.

Still, the South Carolina militia's position was not strong. The militiamen had never seen battle or handled a heavy gun. Cadets manned the unfinished battery on Morris Island.

South Carolina went into an all-out recruiting effort. Their goal was to create a ten-regiment army. That would be an army more than half the size of the whole United States army.

Major Anderson and his men watched all of this war preparation around them. Anderson sent regular reports by mail to Washington about the growing batteries. But the mail to and from Fort Sumter was often delayed and was sometimes opened.

When Governor Pickens received the report from Trescot that the *Harriet Lane* was coming with supplies, Pickens cut off all mail to Fort Sumter. He also ordered the harbor light shut off. Now the beacon on Fort Sumter was the only one in the harbor.

Chapter Four

Star of the West

The rumor about the revenue cutter the *Harriet Lane* coming to Sumter with reinforcements was false. General Scott did order that the *Brooklyn*, a twenty-five gun sloop of war, with four companies "together with extra muskets or rifles, ammunition, and subsistence stores" be made ready as secretly as possible. Once the ship was outfitted, President Buchanan continued to hesitate. The *Brooklyn* waited for orders to sail. Hourly, the South Carolinians tightened their stranglehold on the fort.

In the meantime, General Scott backed down from his decision to send the *Brooklyn*. Maybe they should just send 200 recruits or an unarmed merchant steamer? Finally, the United States government chartered a private side-wheeler, *Star of the West*. It took three days to load the steamer with supplies and 200 men before she left New York.

The newspapers snooped out the story of the *Star of the West* and published articles about reinforcements heading to Charleston. When he received the news, an enraged Secretary of the Interior Thompson sent two telegrams to South Carolina warning the governor that the *Star of the West* was coming. Then he resigned from President Buchanan's cabinet.

To add to the confusion, one of Major Anderson's reports to Secretary of War Joseph Holt about the tightening noose of forts and troops encircling Fort Sumter slipped by the censors. When he read the message, Holt was shocked. The federal government had ordered an unarmed merchant ship to sail into a battery of guns. He dashed off a telegram to stop the *Star of the West* in the New York harbor. But it had already sailed.

Secretary of the Navy Isaac Toucey sent orders to the *Brooklyn* to give aid and to protect the *Star of the West*. But the *Brooklyn* was not to cross the bar into the Charleston harbor. General Scott sent a message to Anderson telling him to fire on the South Carolina batteries if the relief boat was attacked. The message was sent by regular mail and never reached Anderson.

On January 8, Captain Foster's men went into Charleston and brought back a copy of the *Charleston Mercury*. Major Anderson learned from the secessionist paper that the *Star of the West* was heading his way with reinforcements. However, neither Anderson nor any of his officers could be sure about the report. The radical pro-secessionist *Mercury* often spread false rumors. Anderson felt certain General Scott would not send reinforcements without letting him know.

Unknown to Major Anderson, the *Star of the West* had already arrived and was waiting beyond the harbor sandbar, unable to enter until daylight.

At first light, the *Star of the West* started into the harbor, American flag flying, with the soldiers hiding below deck. The captain had no idea that the South Carolinians knew they were coming. The mission was supposed to be secret. But Governor Pickens had received several telegrams warning him of the ship. The South Carolina militia were on the watch.

As the ship entered the harbor, a small South Carolina steamer plying the harbor burned a red and blue signal. When the *Star of the West* was two miles from Sumter, the Morris Island battery began firing. A cannon ball fell short of the steamer, another roared over her.

On the parapet of Fort Sumter, Captain Doubleday focused his spyglass and saw the ship with the Stars and Stripes flying. He saw the shots fired by the South Carolina battery and shouted for Major Anderson.

Major Anderson raced to the parapet, and every man in the garrison lined the walls. They saw the United States ship and the battery's shots. The men itched to fire back. Captain Doubleday expected Anderson to give the order to fire at any minute.

Major Anderson held back. General Scott's message telling him to return fire had never reached him. He had orders to remain strictly on the defensive. He did not want to make a snap decision. Maybe the battery had fired without authority. The guns continued to fire at the ship.

Then the guns from Fort Moultrie began to fire as the ship came into their range. Anderson ordered two 24-pounders aimed at Fort Moultrie but withheld the order to fire. Captain Foster raged because the United States flag had been fired upon and they were not responding.

Aboard the *Star of the West,* the captain knew he was in a bad position. He would have to sail even closer to Fort Moultrie's guns to reach Fort Sumter. And Sumter was not giving him protection. When he saw a South Carolina schooner bearing down on him, the captain ordered the *Star of the West* to turn around. The merchant ship raced back out of the harbor.

After the *Star of the West* disappeared out to sea, the officers of Fort Sumter met in Anderson's quarters. Captains Foster, Doubleday, Seymour, and Crawford were very angry and thought Major Anderson had made a mistake. They felt their lack of action was shameful.

Major Anderson was enraged, too. But he felt it had taken more self-control to refuse to strike back. He revealed to his officers that his orders were to remain on the defensive. It would have meant war to fire on Fort Moultrie and would have been a breach of his orders.

In the meantime, the *Brooklyn,* that was supposed to defend the *Star of the West,* had not yet sailed. When at last she did leave, she failed to locate the *Star of the West* and returned home. The entire mission had been a farce, ruined by the lack of will and indecision of President

General Winfield Scott's communications to Major Anderson were blocked by Charleston secessionists.

Buchanan and the other leaders in Washington.

As Anderson defended his refusal to fire, the South Carolina military leaders met to advise Governor Pickens about their actions. They wanted additional heavy batteries to be built on Sullivan's, James, and Morris Islands.

Governor Pickens sent his newly appointed secretary of state of the republic of South Carolina out to Fort Sumter with a request to surrender the fort. The only answer Major Anderson could give was "No." It was up to the United States government to say if the fort should be surrendered. He did not have authority to make this decision.

Two days after the *Star of the West* had tried and failed to come to Fort Sumter's aid, South Carolina steamers towed four stone-loaded old hulks of ships to the entrance of the channel and sank them. Now no deep-hulled United States war vessels could enter. The noose around Sumter grew tighter.

Slaves were put to work on the South Carolina battery construction. They worked by day and by torchlight at night. On Sullivan's Island, at Fort Johnson on James Island, and on Morris Island new gun installations sprang up. A huge new battery was built on the tip of Morris Island at Cummings Point. The South Carolinians also set to work building a floating battery in the harbor with its guns pointed toward Fort Sumter.

The soldiers in the cold fort could only watch the noose tighten. Captain Doubleday complained bitterly in a letter to his wife in New York that Anderson was letting the South Carolinians surround them. He even hinted darkly that Anderson's southern sympathies were making him act in a suspicious manner.

The garrison struggled to mount fifty-one guns to point at Morris Island, Fort Moultrie, Johnson Island, and Charleston. They removed the flat slabs of stone on the parade ground so that shells fired at them would bury themselves in the sand rather than send sharp bits of rock flying in the sky.

Captain Foster had the men lay mines around the wharf. They built a stone wall to protect the main gate. A howitzer, a short cannon, was mounted at the entrance to fire toward the wharf. Fougasses—piles of stone containing a magazine of gunpowder that could be detonated from inside the fort—were placed along the wall. Captain Seymour invented "flying fougasses" that could be pushed off the tops of the walls and exploded when they fell on the ground.

The provisions brought from Fort Moultrie were dwindling fast. Supplies of sugar, salt, coffee, candles, and soap were growing short. They did have plenty of water in the cisterns and several barrels of salt pork.

In addition to hunger, the coldest part of the winter settled in, and chilly rain and fog seeped into the fort. The soldiers, workmen, wives, and children were cold. In the hurry to leave Fort Moultrie, they had not taken enough coal and had to burn pieces of the construction shacks for heat. Even when the sun shone, it could only reach over the high walls for a few hours. Everyday, Fort Sumter felt more and more like a prison.

On February 1, Major Anderson wrote to Governor Pickens and asked that the women and children be allowed to leave. Governor Pickens agreed. When the ship taking their families to New York left the fort, the men ran to the top of the ramparts. They fired a gun and gave three cheers as a farewell, happy to see their families headed to safety. But then sadness crept in. They might never see their loved ones again.

Governor Pickens sent his attorney, Isaac Hayne, to Washington to ask President Buchanan to *sell* Fort Sumter to South Carolina. Secretary of State Holt answered that, "The President can no more sell and transfer Fort Sumter to South Carolina than he can sell the Capitol of the United States."

Chapter Five

The Federal Government is Dead

By the end of January, five more states had seceded: Mississippi on January 9, Florida on January 10, Alabama on January 11, Georgia on January 19, and Louisiana on January 26. Texas would secede on February 23.

On February 4, delegates from the six seceded states met in Montgomery, Alabama, to form a new government they called the Confederate States of America. They wanted to write a constitution and name a chief executive before March 4 when Abraham Lincoln would be inaugurated. They also wanted to gain some control over the hotheads in Charleston, who they feared would force them into a war before the new government was ready.

The Confederate delegates knew the leaders of the border states were watching them. They wanted the border states, especially Virginia, to join them. Pro-union sentiment was stronger in the border states than it was in the Deep South. Any rash act would only strengthen the hands of the unionists in the border states.

In the Confederate constitution, slavery was made a permanent institution that was fully protected in any new territories the Confederate States of America might acquire. Ironically, the constitution did not give its member states the right to secede from the Confederacy.

After debate, all six delegations voted to make Jefferson Davis, former United States Senator from Mississippi, the first President of the Confederate States of America. Davis had been born within a few months and a few miles of Abraham Lincoln in Kentucky. Tall and erect, he had graduated from West Point and was one of the heroes of the Mexican War. He had hoped to be chosen to lead the southern military forces and was reluctant to take the presidency. His wife said he spoke of the job as someone might speak of a death sentence.

Although Davis thought a war was inevitable, many of the delegates were hopeful that their separation from the Union would be peaceful. They hurried to take the situation in the Charleston harbor out of the hands of the Fire-Eaters now that South Carolina was no longer an independent republic.

The Confederate States appointed Pierre Gustave Toutant Beauregard to take over Charleston's defenses. Beauregard, a small, slender Louisianian whose French family could be traced back to the thirteenth century, had been a captain in the U.S. Army. Now he was a general in the Confederate Army. As were many of the Confederate officers, he was a hero in the Mexican War.

Jefferson Davis was named president of the Confederacy.

Beauregard was a handsome man with graying hair that he kept glossy black with hair dye. One of Major Anderson's former students at West Point, he was an artillery specialist.

General Beauregard studied the harbor fortifications. Fort Sumter stood in the harbor like the Rock of Gibraltar. If fully garrisoned, it would be impregnable. But it was not fully garrisoned. One of Beauregard's jobs was to make sure it remained weak. He repositioned the guns to seal up the harbor rather than just pointing at the fort. Batteries were placed where the guns of Fort Sumter could not reach them. Special trains from Richmond, Virginia, brought mortars, shot, shells, and ammunition.

Throughout the South, militias seized federal arsenals with their stores of arms and ammunition, custom-houses, and revenue cutters. Early in 1861, militias seized Fort Pulaski at Savannah, Georgia; Fort Morgan at Mobile, Alabama; and Fort Barrancas at Pensacola, Florida, along with nineteen posts in Texas. At last, the only coastal forts that remained in federal hands were the forts in the Charleston harbor and Fort Pickens off the Florida coast.

As March 4 neared, Abraham Lincoln began his journey from Springfield, Illinois, to the nation's capitol. Although he was highly respected within the Republican Party, Lincoln was unknown to a great deal of the population. A prominent attorney in Springfield, Lincoln had served one term in the U.S. House of Representatives during the Mexican War. He had first gained the nation's

Confederate General P. G. T. Beauregard was responsible for the defense of Charleston.

attention because of a series of debates held during his campaign against Democratic Senator Stephen Douglas. Lincoln lost the election, but the debates gave him an opportunity to speak on his careful analysis of the history of slavery in America. He argued forcibly that while the founding fathers had clearly recognized slavery in the areas that it currently existed, they had not provided for its extension into new lands acquired by the growing republic. Lincoln had been unwavering in his insistence that slavery should be contained.

Most delegates had arrived at the 1860 Republican Convention in Chicago, Illinois, expecting to nominate William Seward of New York to be their candidate for president. But Seward, a wily man, had made many enemies in the party. Some considered him too radical, others thought he was not radical enough. In short, Seward had been around too long. The party leaders wanted a candidate who would appeal to more moderate voters. Lincoln, through skillful manipulation of events, emerged as the consensus candidate and won the nomination. Seward took the defeat hard, but he consoled himself by thinking that he would be the real power in any Republican Administration, especially one led by a little known lawyer from the edge of the frontier. Many nodded their heads, some with relief, when Lincoln gave Seward the top cabinet position, Secretary of State, of his new administration.

As Abraham Lincoln left Springfield, he spoke from

the back of the train: "I now leave, not knowing when, or whether ever, I may return, with a task before me greater than that which rested upon Washington."

When Lincoln reached Philadelphia, warnings came that he would be murdered in Baltimore. General Scott was responsible for Lincoln's safety. Private detective Allan Pinkerton covered the security details and insisted that Lincoln sneak into Washington in the dead of night. When news of Lincoln's inglorious entry into the city leaked to the newspapers, he became an object of ridicule. Who was this coward, sneaking into town in the middle of the night, who thought he could run the federal government? It looked as thought Seward's plans on running the country might come to pass.

Lincoln found the people of the capital city to be dreary and frightened. Like the nation, Washington seemed to be falling apart. Every day, southern congressman left and soldiers resigned to join the Confederate Army. Two days before Lincoln was inaugurated, Senator Wigfall of Texas stood up in the United States Senate and proclaimed, "This Federal Government is dead."

When Abraham Lincoln was inaugurated on cloudy, raw March 4, 1861, the United States had seven less states than when he was elected. Lincoln proclaimed in his inaugural address that secession was illegal. He insisted that the seven states were not out of the Union and could never go out on their own accord.

Lincoln vowed to hold the federal possessions in the

South. "The power confided in me will be used to hold, occupy and possess the property and places belonging to the government," Lincoln said. Everyone knew he was talking about Fort Sumter.

When he returned to the White House to begin work, Lincoln found a message waiting for him. Two hours before his presidency was over, Buchanan had received a dispatch from Major Anderson. The major said he could not stay at Fort Sumter without supplies. He also reported that Beauregard had mounted so many guns around the harbor that it would take 20,000 troops to reinforce Fort Sumter.

President Lincoln decided to dispatch three men to Charleston to gather firsthand information. Gustavus Fox went to Fort Sumter and met with Anderson. Fox suggested that small boats could reach the fort at night with the needed supplies. Anderson thought the guns at Fort Moultrie and the guard steamers would prevent that. Major Anderson also asked Fox to tell the president that his troops could not stay at Fort Sumter beyond April 15. They were almost out of food.

The second man Lincoln sent south was Stephen Hurlbut, who was to find out if the majority of people of Charleston wanted to secede. It had been suggested that secession was the work of a few powerful hotheads and that the majority of people were still loyal to the Union. Hurlbut found no feelings of national patriotism in South Carolina. He also told the president that Beauregard would stop any boat, even one with bacon and hardtack,

President Abraham Lincoln completed all of his paperwork and correspondence with the help of only two aides.

that tried to come to Fort Sumter.

Ward Lamon was the third man the president sent south. Lamon was sympathetic to the South and he managed to give Anderson the impression that the troops at Fort Sumter would be withdrawn.

Although the reports he received were not hopeful, President Lincoln did not want to give up Fort Sumter. No withdrawal order was sent.

In the meantime, the new Secretary of State, William Seward, forged ahead with his own plans. Seward did not want to reinforce or resupply Fort Sumter. He thought the fort should be surrendered. Seward had influence over Army Chief of Staff General Winfield Scott, and he encouraged the aging Scott to cooperate with his plans. Scott knew that the army was not ready for a war and agreed to advise Lincoln to evacuate Fort Sumter.

Seward thought that war should be avoided and that the president should look for ways to inspire unionist sympathies in the South. Maybe if Lincoln ordered troops to invade Cuba, an enthusiastic wave of patriotic expansionism would seize southern imaginations and the Confederate states would join in the effort. Seward wanted time to develop his plans and hoped to avoid a conflict over Fort Sumter.

Serious discussion of evacuation shocked most of President Lincoln's new cabinet. No one, except Seward, wanted to give in to the Confederacy. But only one cabinet member wanted to send relief to Major Anderson.

The others seemed to suggest doing nothing. This lack of unity and indecisiveness convinced some observers that the new administration was not much different than the previous one.

Seward attempted to force the issue. On March 15, he told Associate Justice John Campbell from Alabama that Fort Sumter would be evacuated in three days. He knew the word would be carried back to the new Confederate government in Montgomery. Seward's leak soon appeared in the newspapers. The Washington correspondent for the *New York Herald* wrote, "I am able to state positively that the abandonment of Fort Sumter has been determined upon by the President and his Cabinet."

Chapter Six

Shelled Out or Starved Out

Inside Fort Sumter, sixty-eight enlisted men, eight musicians, nine officers, and forty-three workmen grew bored. The gunners decided to see if their biggest gun, a ten-inch Columbiad, could fire a shell to Charleston, 5,500 yards away. The gun's range was only 4,828 yards, but they hoped to gain distance by making the shell not quite round and mounting the gun as a mortar.

They only put in two pounds of powder (the full charge was eighteen pounds) and touched it off. The blind shell (one without an explosive charge inside) arched above the harbor, headed for the city. The soldiers watched the shell with awe. The shot neared Charleston. At last it fell—almost on the wharves.

A South Carolina guard boat steamed out immediately. Were they ready to start the war? Major Anderson apologized. It was a practice shot, he assured them. The guard boat left. The Fort Sumter soldiers grinned, satisfied their shots could reach Charleston, if necessary.

Several days later one of the big Confederate 24-pounders on Cummings Point of Morris Island responded by sending a shot toward Fort Sumter. The big ball nicked a corner of the fort, sending pieces of rock flying and splashed close to the Sumter wharf. The men leapt to their guns. A Confederate major apologized for the "accident."

At last, the mail boat from Charleston brought a newspaper to Fort Sumter. The *Charleston Courier* headline said, "THE EVACUATION OF FORT SUMTER DETERMINED ON." The garrison saw that the work on the fortifications around the harbor had ceased, so the news must be true. Then they heard that Senator Wigfall, still in Washington, had sent a telegram that said Anderson would be ordered to evacuate in five days.

Major Anderson had received no such notification. But he was thankful the new president had decided not to attempt to reinforce him and ignite a war. Captain Foster received engineering instructions from Washington about how to prepare for evacuation. The men at Fort Sumter began packing. They had lived through sixteen weeks of mounting tension. "We shall certainly leave on Saturday," one soldier wrote.

General Beauregard was thankful, too, when he heard the news. He did not want to fire on his old teacher. He wrote to tell Major Anderson that no "formal surrender" would be required when Anderson evacuated the fort. He did not want Anderson to suffer the humiliation.

While the garrison waited for evacuation orders, Major

Anderson continued to send his reports to Colonel Samuel Cooper, Adjutant General of the Army. He did not know that Colonel Cooper had resigned. Lincoln's new Secretary of War, Simon Cameron, sent no word to Anderson.

In the North, rumors that Fort Sumter would be evacuated set off strong protests. Encouraged, Jefferson Davis sent commissioners to Washington, D.C., to negotiate for Fort Sumter and Fort Pickens.

In Washington, Seward continued to advocate the evacuation of Fort Sumter. His principal rival in the cabinet, Secretary of the Treasury Salmon P. Chase, who had been Seward's bitter rival for years, warned the president that he would resign if Fort Sumter were surrendered. He argued that this was the place to take a stand against secession. If the president backed down at Sumter, Chase argued, the morale in the North would be destroyed.

Torn between this conflicting advice, President Lincoln wavered. As the president worried, Seward assured the commissioners, through secret channels, that Sumter would soon be turned over to them.

Conditions grew worse inside the fort. Anderson ordered the men to tear down and burn the third construction shack to keep warm. The steady diet of salt pork grew sickening. Lieutenant Hall added up the remaining food: two-thirds barrel of flour, five barrels of hard bread, less than a barrel of rice, one hundred pounds of sugar, twenty-five pounds of coffee, one-sixth barrel of salt, twenty-four barrels of salt pork, two barrels of vinegar, forty

Secretary of State William Seward advocated the removal of federal troops from Fort Sumter.

to the Charleston harbor to protect the *Baltic*. Three steam tugs, *Yankee*, *Uncle Ben*, and *Thomas Freeborn* were hired to help the warships cross the bar at the mouth of Charleston harbor.

Seward continued with his private plan to reinforce Fort Pickens, off the Florida coast. Because of the limited amount of ships, supplies, and soldiers available, the more men and material sent to Fort Pickens, the less there would be for the Sumter expedition. Without informing the secretary of the navy, Seward signed up men and supplies from the meager sources. Seward wanted to send the *Powhatan* to Fort Pickens, so he went to the president for his signature on the requisition order. Lincoln, who was overwhelmed with paperwork and had only two young men as secretaries, did not realize he was signing two different orders for the same warship. Now Seward had presidential permission to send the *Powhatan* to Pensacola, Florida. When the mistake was discovered, President Lincoln ordered the *Powhatan* restored to the Sumter expedition and told Seward to advise the captain of this decision, but Seward delayed. The captain, believing he was acting on the president's final orders, sailed for Pensacola rather than Charleston.

President Lincoln was unaware that his orders regarding the *Powhatan* had not been carried out. On April 8, he sent Governor Pickens a message. Lincoln's personal messenger handed Governor Pickens a small piece of paper:

Gustavus Fox planned the mission to resupply federal troops at Fort Sumter.

I am directed by the President of the United States
to notify you to expect an attempt will be made to
supply Fort Sumter with provisions only, and that
if such attempt be not resisted, no effort to throw
in men, arms or ammunition will be made, without
further notice, or in case of an attack upon the fort.

Pickens was stunned, then enraged. He, along with
most South Carolinians, had been lulled by Seward into
believing Sumter would be evacuated. They all thought
that Seward was the real power in Washington and had
believed what he told the commissioners. This was even
more proof that the "Black Republicans" were untrust-
worthy. The Confederate commissioners in Washington
who had been dealing with Seward returned home fuming
about "Yankee treachery."

When he received the word of Lincoln's decision to
resupply, Senator Wigfall finally resigned his Senate seat
and hurried to Charleston. He wanted to be in on the fight.
He spoke to a crowd in Charleston, saying, "Whether
Major Anderson shall be shelled out or starved out is a
question merely of expediency. We have a new flag; that
flag has not yet been baptized in blood . . . If you think
this is going to be gained without blood. I think you are
mistaken."

Edmund Ruffin, one of the hottest of the hotheads,
urged South Carolina to "strike a blow." The Fire-Eaters
wanted to seize the opportunity to cement the Confederacy with action.

Fox sailed for Fort Sumter on April 10. He carried 200 recruits and enough supplies to keep Fort Sumter going for a year. What he did not know was that the *Powhatan*, the biggest ship of the expedition, the one he was depending on for defense of his flotilla, was on its way to Pensacola, Florida.

Major Anderson received notification of Fox's supply expedition through the regular mail on April 4. This was the first communication of any kind he had received from Secretary of War Cameron, who wrote: "You will hold out, if possible, till the arrival of the expedition."

Cameron's instructions deflated Major Anderson's hopes of peace. He knew the attempt to reinforce Fort Sumter meant war. He wrote back to Secretary Cameron: "I fear that its [the expedition's] result cannot fail to be disastrous to all concerned." His report never reached Cameron.

Anderson's men welcomed the news of the relief expedition with rousing cheers. They knew the southerners would not let the supply ship into the harbor. They would finally have their chance to fight. They were determined to hold out until the *Baltic* arrived.

Each morning and evening the men and officers received one cracker to eat. They added this to their slim rations of hard bread, salt pork, and water. The men found some rice in a storage room where a glass window had shattered from an exploding practice shell. They sifted the damp, mouldy rice to remove the glass and added it to their food supplies. Surgeon Captain Crawford found a potato (he said in his diary that it was "tramped on but not hurt much") and added that to the food. The men grew weak from the poor diet and tried to conserve their energy. Surgeon Captain Crawford arranged his hospital facilities.

The garrison's supply of one vital item, paper cartridge bags used to make explosives, was very low. They cut up their blankets and extra shirts, sewed them into cartridge bags, and filled them with measured charges of powder.

The men inside the fort had no illusions about their ability to hold on for an extended time even if they had plenty of food. General Beauregard had built a "circle of fire" around Fort Sumter. Seven thousand men surrounded the 128 men in Fort Sumter. Captain Foster did a calculation of the enemy's batteries:

> On Sullivan's Island: Floating battery protected behind a seawall at west end of island—two 42-pounders and two 32-pounders; next, the powerful Dahlgren; next, two 32-pounders and two 24-pounders; west of Fort Moultrie—three ten-inch mortars; in Fort Moultrie—three eight-inch Columbiads, two eight-inch seacoast howitzers, five 32-pounders and four 24-pounders. On the mainland behind Sullivan's Island: two ten-inch mortars. On James Island: at Fort Johnson—one 24-pounder; south of this—four ten-inch mortars. On Morris Island: a battery of two 24-pounders

and one rifled Blakely gun that could throw a 10-pound shot with accuracy; a battery of four ten-inch Columbiads; and a battery of three ten-inch mortars.

Captain Foster knew the Confederate batteries had hotshot furnaces. With furnaces, the cannon balls could be heated until they became red-hot coals. When the balls were fired into wooden structures, the buildings erupted in flames.

Major Anderson ordered everyone to move their bed-rolls to the bombproof casemates (armored, brick-walled gunrooms). The wooden barracks were too vulnerable. They would live and fight in the casemates.

Chapter Seven

Open Fire!

April 11 dawned cloudy with a slight breeze. At first light, the Fort Sumter garrison discovered that a floating battery, a huge barge with cannon, had been towed to the western end of Sullivan's Island where its guns bore directly on Fort Sumter. It was in a position to attack on the side of the fort where the relief boat would approach.

The food supply that Lieutenant Hall had tabulated was nearly gone. That day the remaining hard bread was eaten. Only a few crackers and some salt pork remained.

By 3:00 P.M., no relief ship had appeared at the entrance to the harbor. But a small boat with a white flag was approaching from Charleston. Two of Beauregard's aides jumped from the boat and were taken to Major Anderson. They handed him a message from Beauregard:

> I am ordered by the Government of the Confederate States to demand the evacuation of Fort Sumter . . . All proper facilities will be afforded for the removal of yourself and your command,

together with the company arms and property. The flag which you have upheld so long and with so much fortitude, under the most trying circumstances, may be saluted by you on taking it down."

Major Anderson asked his officers to come with him to another room. He read Beauregard's message to his officers. They unanimously refused to give up the fort.

Anderson reported the decision to Beauregard's aides and told them they would wait for the first shot. "And if you do not batter us to pieces, we shall be starved out in a few days," he added.

When the aides repeated Anderson's words to General Beauregard, he notified Confederate President Jefferson Davis by telegraph. Davis told Beauregard to check on the facts. If the men in the fort were almost out of food, there would be no need to fire on the fort.

Once more, the Confederate messengers delivered a letter to Major Anderson. It was after midnight, 12:45 A.M. on April 12, when they arrived back at the fort. Beauregard wanted to know exactly how long the Fort Sumter garrison could hold out.

Major Anderson called his officers together again. Their best judgment was that the garrison could hold out five more days, three of those days would be without food.

Major Anderson wrote a reply to Beauregard. He stated that the U.S. Army garrison would evacuate the fort on April 15 *if* General Beauregard would provide transportation, *if* the Confederates did not commit a hostile act against the fort or the United States flag, and *if* new orders or supplies were not received from the United States government.

The Confederate messengers read the reply. They decided not to row back to Charleston for an answer. Anderson's terms were unacceptable. They replied to Major Anderson in writing: "By authority of Brigadier General Beauregard we have the honor to notify you that he will open the fire of his batteries on Fort Sumter in one hour from this time." It was 3:20 in the morning of April 12, 1861.

In the dark, a circle of flickering campfires surrounded Fort Sumter. Beauregard had put his men on alert at midnight. The hotshot furnaces glowed, waiting for shot to heat. Along the sand dunes of Morris Island, Confederate sentries watched for the supply boat and the armed boatloads of Yankees they were certain would accompany it. Out in the dark water Confederate boats cruised, ready to set off blue rocket flares if they spotted any ships.

Eccentric Edmund Ruffin had volunteered as a gunner. He vowed to man his post until the Confederate flag floated over Fort Sumter. He was stationed in the iron battery on Cummings Point on Morris Island with the heavy-duty Columbiads. The night before, the company had decided that fiery old Ruffin should have the honor of firing the first shot of the war he had hoped for so long. Ruffin slept restlessly in his uniform that night.

Edmund Ruffin, a native Virginian and fertilizer developer, fired the first shot at Fort Sumter.

Drums woke the men on Morris Island at 4:00 A.M. They ran to their stations. Ruffin, six feet tall, slender and straight, his uniform buttoned to his throat, hurried to his gun.

At 4:30 A.M. on April 12, 1861, Captain George S. James fired the signal gun from Fort Johnson on James Island. A flash of light, a dull explosion, and the shell arched over the water, glowing red in the night sky and exploding over Fort Sumter.

After the signal gun was fired, Ruffin pulled the lanyard of his cannon, firing the first shot from his battery. Then, all along the harbor and from all the forts, sheets of flame flashed out. The sky became like a night of holiday fireworks. People in Charleston trooped up to the rooftops and along the waterfront to watch the show. The rumbling, deadening roar of the Confederate artillery filled the air.

But Fort Sumter lay silent. No guns fired. The Confederates wondered if Anderson had decided to quit without a fight. When dawn came, though, the American flag was still flying proudly over the fort.

Inside the fort, reveille was at 6:00 A.M. The men ate a two-course breakfast, fat pork and water, and then fell in at assembly. Major Anderson informed them that they would use only the guns on the lower casemate level. These guns fired solid shot.

The men groaned. All of the shell guns were on the barbette tier. After they had worked so hard to mount the

Charleston townspeople climbed to their rooftops to witness the first battle of the Civil War.

heaviest artillery on the barbette, where they could fire over the parapet of the fort, now they would not use them. But Major Anderson told them it was too dangerous on the parapet and he did not want to risk their lives. The heaviest guns in the lower casemates were three 42-pounders.

Finally, just after 7:00 A.M., Captain Abner Doubleday proudly gave the order to commence firing. His men fired a 32-pounder. The shot, aimed at the battery on Morris Island at Cummings Point where Edmund Ruffin had fired the first shot, struck the ironclad slanted roof of the battery and bounced off. Frustrated, Doubleday's men poured more shots at Morris Island.

Lieutenant Jefferson C. Davis, who took much kidding from the soldiers because he shared his name with the Confederate president, ordered his men to fire their mortars at James Island. Captain Crawford's men, meanwhile, shot at the floating battery that was hiding behind a rock seawall near Fort Moultrie.

The Sumter guns did not have breech sights. Makeshift vertical marking rods supplied the gunners with an elevation marker. Sometimes the men stuck their heads up and watched where their balls struck so they could correct their aim with the next shot.

Four men manned each gun. Each team worked in rhythm—sponge the barrel, load cartridge, ram it, load ball and wad, ram it, and fire. The forty-two workmen carried ammunition and powder to the guns.

Inside Fort Sumter, it sounded like a huge, continuous thunderstorm. Metal whined and ricocheted around the parade ground. Chunks of walls were blasted off and sailed across the sky. Confederate shells continuously exploded inside the fort and up on the parapet.

Inside the bomb proof casemates, the Fort Sumter men were comparatively safe. But while the heavy Confederate guns pounded Fort Sumter, the smaller guns fired from the casemates did little harm to the Confederate batteries. The gunners scored good hits, right on target, but the small balls bounced off. The heavy guns mounted on the parapet hurled 65- and 128-pound shells. They would have dealt out serious damage to the Confederate fortifications, but the men did not dare go up to use them. With the 32- and 42-pounders, it was as if the Fort Sumter gunners attacked the Confederates with peashooters.

When the Fort Sumter gunners turned their barrels toward Fort Moultrie, their shots landed in bags of sand and bales of cotton. The cotton and sand had been stacked many feet thick around the fort. One Fort Sumter shot did smash into The Moultrie House, a hotel where spectators crowded on the porch. The sightseers scattered for safety.

The bombardment raged on. At noon, Major Anderson ordered that only six guns could fire: two at Fort Moultrie, two at Cummings Point, and two at the batteries on the west end of Sullivan's Island. The garrison only had 700 cartridge bags at the beginning of the firing, and they were blown apart faster than the men could sew them. They hurried to sew more cartridge bags from whatever material they could find.

One soldier sneaked up to the barbette and fired every gun pointed toward Fort Moultrie by himself. Then two sergeants climbed up and fired a ten-inch Columbiad at Cummings Point. The first shot was too high. They aimed again and shot. Too low. And with the recoil from the second shot the 7.5 ton gun hurled in a backwards somersault off its carriage and crashed below the barbette, nearly crushing one man.

Then red-hot shots began raining into the fort. The roofs of the tall wooden barracks caught fire. The Fort Sumter men quickly formed into a fire-fighting detail, but ten-inch shells burst overhead and redhots streamed in. The fire spread.

Finally, some shells blasted the iron tank cisterns under the barracks roof and water poured over the fires. The fires sputtered and began sending up clouds of pungent, piney smoke that drifted into the casemates, choking the men inside.

The garrison ran out of fuses to fire the mortars. They tried to improvise fuses, but they would not work. Then a heavy rain began to fall.

As the day wore on, the garrison continued to pray for the arrival of the relief expedition. Surely, it would come soon. It should have been there by the 11th or 12th.

At last, lookouts at the fort spotted the ships. They began to shout. The United States war ships were just beyond the bar. Two ships steamed closer with the United States flag flying. Major Anderson ordered the soldiers to dip the flag to acknowledge the ships. As it was lowered, an enemy shot cut the rope. The flag stuck at half-mast.

New spirit filled the men even as their fort continued to burn and smoke. At dark, Major Anderson ordered a cease-fire. They did not have any cartridges to waste.

Anderson reasoned that the ships would deliver their cargo under the cover of night. He and Captain Foster directed the preparations for the boats with supplies and men. They realized it would be difficult to identify boats that came by night. They would not be able to tell the difference between friends and enemies.

The men finished the preparations. Midnight came, but no relief boats arrived. Major Anderson ordered his men to rest. At sea, a storm raged.

Chapter Eight

You Are On Fire

The storm scattered the relief vessels as they approached Charleston. When Captain Gustavus Fox of the *Baltic* finally steamed up to the bar at the mouth of the harbor to make his run for Fort Sumter, he found only the warship *Pawnee* and the five-gun, paddle-wheeler *Harriet Lane* waiting to assist him. Unknown to Fox, the tug *Thomas Freeborn* had never left New York and the *Uncle Ben* had washed ashore in the storm and was seized by the Confederates.

Fox determined to make a run for the fort anyway. His orders were to provision Fort Sumter and that was what he intended to do. The *Pawnee* captain refused to go with him. His said that his orders were to wait for the *Powhatan*, which was, unknown to him and Fox, on its way to Florida.

Undeterred, and with only the *Harriet Lane* as an escort, Fox headed into the harbor. As he steamed in, the wind gradually wafted the smell of gunpowder across the harbor. He realized that the war had already begun. His orders to peaceably provision the fort were void.

The captain of the *Pawnee* realized the war had begun, too. His reaction was to change his mind about waiting for the *Powhatan* and to sail into the harbor. If the war had started, he wanted to be part of it. But Fox halted him. They should wait for the 300 men on the *Powhatan,* he said. The three ships turned around and sailed outside the harbor to wait.

The weather turned worse and the wind whipped up a high sea. The recruits on the *Baltic* became seasick. They tried to practice getting in and out of small boats in preparation for a landing party.

Merchant ships also came and anchored beside them, seeking protection from the gale. The Confederates, seeing a number of ships anchored outside the harbor, thought a large federal fleet lay waiting to come in.

The morning of April 13 was foggy. The sea was ugly. Captain Fox said there was no use waiting for the *Powhatan* and decided to send in the reinforcements and supplies with the small boats. But the naval officers told him open boats had no chance of reaching Fort Sumter in the heavy sea.

The U.S.S. *Pocahontas* arrived after noon. Her captain informed Fox that the *Powhatan* was not coming.

Captain Fox then planned a night expedition to reach the fort. But it was too late. The ship's lookouts reported that Fort Sumter's flag was no longer flying.

The men inside Fort Sumter awoke on April 13 and realized no relief boats had come in the night. They ate their breakfast of salt pork and water and began firing their guns again. Unknown to Major Anderson, one of his brothers-in-law was firing at Fort Sumter from Fort Moultrie.

The Iron Battery on Cummings Point began shelling the main gates of Fort Sumter, splintering them and scattering pieces throughout the courtyard. Red-hot shots set the barracks on fire again. As dense smoke rose from Fort Sumter, the Confederates sent more hotshots flying.

The powder storage room was on the main floor of one of the barracks. A trail of spilled gunpowder, which had leaked from the barrels as they were moved from the storage room, snaked a fuse to more than 275 barrels of gunpowder.

While the gun crews kept firing, the rest of the garrison, including the workmen and musicians, ran to haul barrel after barrel out of the barracks and to place them in the casemates. Sparks and burning embers flew about. Major Anderson ordered the casement's copper door shut tight. The door was so hot the men could hardly touch it. But they got it shut and banked dirt against it.

Intense heat reached the stockpiles of shells and grenades. They began exploding, showering the fort and men with fiery debris. One-fifth of the fort was on fire. The splintered main gates burst into flames.

Steady rain and dripping cisterns caused the burning

barracks and storage rooms to smoke like hissing smudge fires. Wind from the gun openings blew blinding smoke back into the casemates. The soldiers had to lay on the floor with wet rags over their faces to try to keep the smoke out of their noses and mouths. In between shots, they gasped for fresh air at the gun openings in the walls. They could hardly see their own guns.

Major Anderson knew the powder stored in the casemates with the gunners could explode soon. He ordered all but five barrels of powder to be dumped out of the gun openings into the harbor. But the tide was low. The barrels swirled together along the shore, settling by the fort. The Confederates turned their guns on the barrels, exploding them and taking out one of Fort Sumter's guns.

The men soaked what blankets they had that had not been used for cartridge bags and covered the remaining powder barrels. When the last five barrels of gunpowder were used up, they would have no more powder for their guns. The soldiers began using socks for cartridge bags. Soon no soldiers had any socks left.

About 1:00 P.M., an enemy shot broke off the flagstaff. The Stars and Stripes flew down and landed on the ground. Hot coals landed on it. Lieutenant Hall dashed out into the fire and exploding shells to snatch up the smoldering flag. The intense heat singed his hair, and the gilt epaulets on his uniform grew so hot he had to rip them off.

Hall, Peter Hart (Major Anderson's aide), Captain

Seymour, and Lieutenant Snyder ran with the battered flag up to the parapet. The enemy must not think the garrison had lowered its flag in surrender. They fastened a pole to a gun carriage and raised the flag again. All the while enemy guns fired steadily at them. They ran back down inside the fort.

Ex-Senator Wigfall, who was watching the action from Cummings Point, commanded a rowboat. He ordered two men to row him out to the fort. With a white flag draped on his sword, he landed on the shore. The main gates were burning, so he turned and climbed in through a gun enclosure.

The gunners stationed there jumped back in surprise as the man barged in out of the smoke. He waved his white flag and demanded to be taken to Major Anderson.

"Your flag is down, you are on fire, and you are not firing your guns," he barked at Lieutenant Davis.

Davis pointed up at the flag flying above the fort. Wigfall ordered Davis to put the white flag up instead. Davis refused. Wigfall turned and waved the white flag out the gun opening.

Major Anderson hurried over to see what was happening. Wigfall told him he had defended his flag nobly but that it was madness to persevere. Fire smoldered everywhere in the burned-out buildings of the fort. The stores of ammunition would probably explode soon; the cartridges were all used up. The parade ground was a shambles of blown-out craters and debris. The walls of

General Beauregard did not know that Louis T. Wigfall (pictured above) had rushed to Fort Sumter and persuaded Major Anderson to surrender.

the fort had suffered 600 direct hits. The parapet was almost destroyed. The main gate was blown and burned away. The Confederates had blasted the fort with more than 3,000 rounds of shot and shell.

Anderson agreed with Wigfall. Further resistance was futile. He had fulfilled all that Washington had asked of him. No relief was coming. Anderson told Wigfall that he had already informed General Beauregard of his terms of evacuation: He would leave the fort with his command, taking all men and arms, and with a salute to the flag. But he would leave now instead of on the 15th.

At 1:30 P.M. on April 13, 1861, thirty-three hours after the first shot was fired, the flag of the United States came down from Fort Sumter.

When General Beauregard saw the United States flag come down, he sent aides out to speak to Anderson. When they arrived, Anderson greeted them and asked them to thank General Beauregard for his kindness. The aides looked at each other. They did not understand what he was talking about. Anderson explained that Colonel Wigfall had just been there by the authority of General Beauregard. Major Anderson had surrendered to him.

The aides informed Anderson that Colonel Wigfall had not seen General Beauregard for two days. He had not been acting on the General's authority.

Major Anderson sighed. This meant the terms of surrender were void. Anderson ordered the white flag of truce lowered. He would raise his flag again and the battle would go on.

The aides conferred and then asked Major Anderson not to start the battle again. They would go to Beauregard and give him a letter stating Anderson's terms. The white flag went up again. All of the guns were silent, waiting.

Three hours later the aides returned. Beauregard had agreed to the terms Anderson had asked for. The surrender of Fort Sumter was official. The Civil War had begun.

Chapter Nine

The Last Salute

Sunday, April 14, 1861, dawned clear. Unlike the stormy seas that had beat back the fleet beyond the bar, gentle waves washed the harbor. It was victory Sunday for the Confederate States of America.

Boatloads of people jammed the Charleston harbor. Sightseers were rowed past the fort at fifty cents a head. Troops and spectators crowded together on the shores of Sullivan's Island, Morris Island, and James Island.

At noon, the men of Fort Sumter gathered on the parade ground for the final ceremony. They had packed what belongings they had left in silence and sadness. Major Anderson was close to tears. General Beauregard did not attend the ceremony. He did not want to add to the distress of his former teacher.

The United States Stars and Stripes was hoisted above the fort. Only three cartridge bags were found. The men had a hard time finding enough material to sew cartridge bags for the 100-gun salute. The gun salute from one of the big guns on the barbette began firing.

Again and again, the big gun boomed. Private Daniel Hough put a cartridge in for another shot. The barrel must not have been completely sponged from the previous shot; embers burned inside. When Hough put in the new cartridge, the gun blew up. Private Hough was killed instantly. He was the first casualty of the battle for Fort Sumter. Another man wounded in the explosion died later.

Private Hough was buried with honors in the fort. By 4:00 P.M., the garrison was ready to leave. Major Anderson, with his head bowed, carried the Sumter flag, torn and burned around the edges. The band played "Yankee Doodle" as the troops marched out of the fort. Near the center of the parade ground was the new grave. The shattered flagstaff sprawled on the ground.

A transport waited to take them out to the fleet anchored beyond the bar. The tired and depressed men were heading north. As they left, the Confederate flag, the Stars and Bars, was raised above Fort Sumter.

Aboard the *Baltic*, Major Anderson reported to Secretary of War Cameron:

> Having defended Fort Sumter for Thirty-four hours, until the quarters were entirely burned, the main gates destroyed by fire, the gorge walls seriously injured, the magazine surrounded by flames, and its door closed from the effects of heat, four barrels and three cartridges of powder only being avail-

able, and no provisions remaining but pork, I accepted terms of evacuation offered by General Beauregard . . . and marched out of the fort Sunday afternoon, the 14th instant, with colors flying and drums beating, bringing away company and private property, and saluting my flag with fifty guns.

Major Anderson, the man the Union hailed as a hero, felt he had failed. But the failure was not Anderson's. The nation had blundered into a terrible war. Two percent of the country's population would die in what remains the bloodiest war ever to occur in the Western Hemisphere.

The United States Navy attacked Fort Sumter two times during the war. On April 9, 1863, a fleet of ironclads, called "monitors" after the original ironclad Union warship *Monitor*, attacked the fort that guarded Charleston harbor. But the heavy and unwieldy ironclads were easily defeated in the shallow harbor waters.

Again, in August of 1863, an ironclad fleet bombarded Fort Sumter. They nearly reduced the fort to rubble, but they never captured it. Fort Sumter stayed in Confederate hands throughout the war.

Anderson's men faced four years of terrible war. They fought in battles from Pennsylvania to Florida, from Virginia to Arkansas. Five of the officers—Doubleday, Foster, Crawford, Seymour, and Davis—became Union generals. Lieutenant Hall became a colonel and led a brigade at Gettysburg. Captain Talbot and Lieutenant Snyder died in the war. Lieutenant Meade of Virginia left the army when his state seceded after Fort Sumter surren-

Major Anderson again raised the United States flag above Fort Sumter at the close of the Civil War.

dered and fought for the Confederacy. He died of illness early in the war.

After four long, bloody years, the Civil War ended at Appomattox Courthouse, Virginia. Confederate General Robert E. Lee surrendered to the Union General Ulysses S. Grant on April 9, 1865. The remainder of the Confederate forces had surrendered by June.

The war's end claimed another victim. Edmund Ruffin, who had fired the first shot at Fort Sumter, killed himself after hearing of Lee's surrender. He said he could not live in a "Black Republican America."

President Lincoln, who had grown from a cautious and indecisive president to a strong leader during the course of the war, ordered that the repossession of Fort Sumter be observed in ceremony. So at noon, on April 14, 1865, exactly four years after he had surrendered, brevet Major General Anderson returned to Fort Sumter. Lincoln had been invited to attend, but he decided to stay in Washington. He planned to attend a production of an English play called *My American Cousin* that night at Ford's Theater with his wife and some friends.

As the ceremonies at Fort Sumter began, Charleston harbor was filled with United States ships, their victory flags flying in the wind. General Anderson entered the fort with his family. He was fifty-nine years old, but he looked much older. He had served as a brigadier general in Kentucky during the war, but he had been so broken by the strain of the siege and battle of Fort Sumter that he never fully recovered. Nevertheless, he carried himself with military straightness. Under his arm he carried the flag his garrison had defended so bravely.

As General Anderson climbed over the crumbling fort wall on a wooden stairway, he was shocked by the ruin. The fort had been reduced to a heap of rubble by the ironclad attacks in 1863. It was mostly an unrecognizable heap of rock, bricks, and charred timbers.

Anderson climbed to the speaker's platform, holding the hand of his six-year old son, Robert Jr. With him were his old soldier companions, Peter Hart, General Doubleday, and Chaplain Mattias Harris, who had led the prayer service the morning Anderson's garrison had occupied Fort Sumter after leaving Fort Moultrie. Captain Fox was there, too. He was now Assistant Secretary of the Navy.

Peter Hart walked forward and fastened their flag to the halyards. Major Anderson rose to speak:

> After four long, long years of bloody war, I restore to its proper place this dear flag which floated here during peace, before the first act of this cruel Rebellion. I thank God that I have lived to see this day and to be here to perform this . . . duty to my country. I thank God who so singly blessed us.

With that, Anderson took the rope and raised the flag. The Stars and Stripes caught the breeze, snapped to attention, and flew over Fort Sumter again.

Epilogue

Abraham Lincoln loved to go to the theater. He found relief from the pressures of the presidency by laughing at the comedies that were often presented on the American stage. On the night of April 14, 1865, he had trouble finding someone to accompany him and the first lady to a production of *My American Cousin* at Ford's Theater. General Ulysses S. Grant and his wife declined an invitation. They wanted to visit their children in New Jersey. Secretary of War Edwin Stanton also refused. He advised Lincoln against going because Washington was full of southern sympathizers angry at defeat, but Lincoln insisted. Finally, he found a young officer, Major Henry R. Rathbone, who escorted his fiancé, Clara Harris.

The president seemed to enjoy the play. He was seen in his box laughing several times. Then, during an especially funny moment in the second scene of the third act, John Wilkes Booth crept quietly into the president's box, pointed a derringer at the back of his head, and fired. It was about 10:15 P.M.

Booth's accomplices tried to kill members of the cabinet, too. Secretary of State William Seward was stabbed and left for dead in his bed. He survived. But the president died at 7:22 the following morning, on April 15, 1865. Booth escaped Ford's Theater, but was tracked down to a Virginia barn where he was shot and killed on April 26.

Glossary

abolitionist: someone who wants to end slavery.

batteries: a set of guns (usually four or six) or other heavy artillery; the emplacement for one or more pieces of artillery.

bar: a ridge, of sand or gravel, on a shore or harbor entrance that is formed by the action of the tides or currents.

barbette: a platform or mound within a fort from which guns are fired over a parapet.

Blakely Rifle: a British army officer, Captain Theophilus Alexander Blakely, pioneered a banding system for rifled cannon. At least five, and possibly as many as ten, types of Blakely rifles were manufactured. The Blakely projectile was one of the first rifled projectiles to be fired at Fort Sumter.

breech: the part of the gun behind the bore.

casemate: an armored compartment for artillery on a rampart.

cistern: a tank for catching and storing rainwater.

case shot: shells with lead or iron balls inside.

colors: a flag or banner of a military unit or country.

Columbiad: a heavy, iron, artillery piece which could fire shot and shell at a high angle of elevation using a heavy powder charge. They were smoothbore guns, usually of large caliber, that had less windage than normal. This gave the gun greater range and accuracy.

Dahlgren: a type of smoothbore gun, designed by John A. B. Dahlgren of the U.S. Navy. It was of much larger diameter at the breech, allowing larger powder charges to be used, giving it its distinctive soda bottle shape.

embrasure: a flared opening for a gun in a wall or parapet.

esplanade: a flat, open stretch of pavement or grass along the shore.

garrison: the troops stationed at a military post or the post itself.

intermediary: one who acts as an agent between persons.

lame duck: an elected officeholder who continues to serve during the period until the inauguration of a successor.

leavings: scraps.

magazine: a supply chamber.

mortars: stubby weapons which fired heavy projectiles in a high arc. Only a small powder charge was needed to project the shot or shell to its maximum elevation.

parade: troops taking part in a ceremonial review; the place of assembly for a review of troops.

parapet: a low, protective wall or railing along the edge of a roof, balcony, or similar structure.

pentagonal: five-sided.

pounder: many weapons were classified by the wight of the projectile fired and were known by "pounder", i.e. 10-pounder, 20-pounder. This was not the weight of the cannon itself.

rampart: a fortification consisting of an elevation or embankment, often provided with a parapet.

rifling: a system of lands and grooves in a barrel which caused a projectile to turn as it exited the muzzle, thereby improving trajectory and accuracy.

secede: leave the union.

shoal: a place in a body of water where the water is particularly shallow.

soundings: measured depth of water.

spike: to render a muzzle loading gun useless by driving a long, thick, sharp-pointed piece of wood or metal into the vent.

treason: betraying one's own country by purposely acting to aid its enemies.

windage: the difference in size between the diameter of shot or shell and the diameter of the gun's bore. The greater the windage, the less accurate the gun.

Websites to Explore

American Civil War. Tuscaloosa, Alabama: Southern Culture Resources, University of Alabama. http://www.lib.ua.edu/smr/south3.htm.

The American Civil War. Features links to other civil war websites. http://www.exepc.com/~kap/cw/.

The American Civil War, the Army of Virginia and the Army of the Potomac, 1861-1865. Rockingham, Virginia: Rockingham County Public Schools. http://www.rockingham.k12.va.us/EMS/CivilWar/CivilWar.html.

The American Civil War Homepage. Knoxville, Tennessee: University of Tennessee. http://sunsite.utk.edu/civil-war/warweb.html.

"The Civil War." *American Battlefield Protection Program.* National Park Service. http://www.cr.nps.gov/abpp/civil.htm.

Military History. National Park Service. http://www.cr.nos.gov/military.htm.

Bibliography

Books

Bishop, Jim. *The Day Lincoln Was Shot*. New York: Gramercy Books, a Division of Random House, 1955.

Catton, Bruce. *America Goes to War: The Civil War and Its Meaning To American History*. Middletown, Connecticut: Wesleyan University Press, 1958.
————. *The American Heritage Picture History of the Civil War*. New York: American Heritage Publishing Co., Inc., 1960.
————. *The Coming Fury*. New York: Doubleday & Company, Inc., 1961.

Davis, William C. and the Editors of Time-Life Books. *The Civil War: First Blood: Fort Sumter to Bull Run*. Alexandria, Virginia: Time-Life Books, 1983.

Foote, Shelby. *The Civil War: Fort Sumter to Perryville*. New York: Random House, 1958.

Hendrick, Burton F. *Lincoln's War Cabinet*. Boston: Little, Brown and Company, 1946.

Hunter, Alvah F. *A Year on a Monitor and the Destruction of Fort Sumter*. Columbia, South Carolina: University of South Carolina Press, 1987.

Kennedy, Frances H., editor, *The Civil War Battlefield Guide*. Boston: Houghton Mifflin Company, 1990.

Kennedy, John F. *Profiles in Courage*. New York: Harper & Row, Publishers, 1956.

Leifermann, Henry. *South Carolina*. Oakland, California: Fodor's Travel Publications, Inc., 1995.

Nevins, Allan. *The Emergence of Lincoln: Prologue to Civil War 1859-1861*. New York: Charles Scribner's Sons, 1950.
————. *The War for the Union: The Improvised War 1861-1862*. New York: Charles Scribner's Sons, 1959.

Stowe, Harriet Beecher. *Uncle Tom's Cabin*. New York: E. P. Dutton & Co., Inc., 1909.

Swanberg, W. A. *First Blood: The Story of Fort Sumter*. New York: Charles Scribner's Sons, 1957.

Wheeler, Richard. *A Rising Thunder: From Lincoln's Election to the Battle of Bull Run: An Eyewitness History*. New York: Harper Collins Publishers, 1994.

Websites

Latner, Richard B.*Crisis at Fort Sumter*. New Orleans, Louisiana: Tulane University. http://www.tulane.edu/~latner/.

Weeks, Dick. *Shotgun's Home of the American Civil War*. http://www.civilwarhome.com/.

Index